Millennium
English
READER IV

Text
Parvathi Krishnan
Indira Subramani

Illustrations
Vidya Saxena

BPI EDUCATIONAL

BPI Educational is an imprint of
Business Publications Inc

ISBN 81-7693-038-5
© BPI Educational, 2000
Copyright permissions have been sought wherever applicable.

Published by

BPI Educational

No. 1 Second Street
Nandanam Extension
Chennai 600 035
© 433 1953 ● 436 3416/17
Email : quartett@md3.vsnl.net.in

Publisher's Note

The *Millennium* English series comprises Readers, Workbooks and Teachers' Manuals. There are two introductory books OA and OB for pre-primary classes and 5 Readers and Workbooks for classes 1 to 5, which constitute the complete primary language development package. The books reflect the current thinking about language learning and syllabus design and also introduce learning strategies to promote learner autonomy.

The Readers are the core books of the series. This Reader focuses on :

■ Texts, mostly in story format, based on cross-curricular and cross-cultural themes.

■ A variety of questions and activities to motivate and create the necessary environment for learning the language.

■ Developing the four basic language skills of listening, speaking, reading and writing.

■ Enriching vocabulary through intensive practise of words in the text and word extension exercises.

■ Enabling activities which lead to a fairly focussed appropriate writing.

■ Recycling language from the earlier unit to aid retention of language.

■ Fun element for a positive reinforcement of the material.

■ Sensitizing the learner to the subtler and finer nuances of life and language through poems.

■ Developing, through the text matter, positive values and attitudes like kindness to animals, preservation of the environment, caring for others, helping one another and respect for the living.

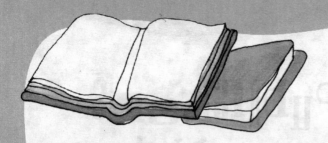

The Format

This book has 8 units. Six of them have a poem, each of which is linked thematically to the reading text in the unit. An attempt has been made to sensitize the learner to the finer nuances of language through the poems. They are introduced to some simple poetic devices like rhyme, rhythm, simile, alliteration and metaphor.

The reading texts have seven distinctive sections

- Think (stimulates learning)
- Help to Understand (develops reading skills)
- Useful Words (enriches and extends vocabulary)
- Language in Use (from class 4: serves as a framework for usage in language structure)
- Before You Write (helps with the process of writing)
- Now Write (provides for appropriate writing)
- Game Time (helps consolidate learning)

The Teachers' Manual provides step by step back up for the Reader. Model question papers for effective evaluation of the skills learnt have been provided in the Teachers' Manual.

Suggestions to the teacher

- Read the Teachers' Manual before you start the course.
- Make lesson planning an integral part of your teaching.
- Make full use of the help provided in the Manual to ensure that both you and your students derive the maximum benefit from the *Millennium* English Reader 4.

It is sincerely hoped that this course will make teaching and learning of language an enjoyable, fun experience and help equip the learner with the success skills required to meet the demands and challenges of present day academics.

Contents

	1 Human Nature	2 People	3 Hobbies	4 Environment
Think	☛ Travel Preparation ☛ Discussion – Qualities of a Friend	☛ Associated Words ☛ Remembering Dates and People	☛ Feelings for Books ☛ Talking about Indoor/Outdoor Games	☛ Discussion – A World without Trees ☛ About Air Pollution
Poem	☛ A Song About Myself	☛ My Own Mother	☛ Books	☛ My Tree
Read	☛ Two Friends	☛ Remembering Gandhiji – A Child Like Us	☛ Chess	☛ Stop the Smoke Please! We want to live
Help to Understand	☛ Questions Answers ☛ Sentence completion ☛ Table completion	☛ Questions Answers	☛ Yes / No Answers ☛ Fill in the blanks ☛ Matching exercise ☛ Questions Answers	☛ Sentence completion ☛ Questions Answers ☛ Fill in the blanks ☛ True / False
Useful Words	☛ Find words for given meaning ☛ Comparative form of adjectives	☛ Word Connotations ☛ Prefixes, Suffixes	☛ Match words to meaning ☛ Homophones	☛ Word associations ☛ Matching word to meaning ☛ Sound words
Language in Use	☛ Conditional sentences	☛ Phrasal Verbs	☛ Making Requests ☛ Giving Instructions	☛ Usage phrases/ expressions
Before You Write	☛ Collecting adjectives to describe a person	☛ Listing Good / Bad habits	☛ Learning to write – how to play a game	☛ Brainstorm for Ideas
Now Write	☛ Description of a Friend	☛ Code of Conduct ☛ 2 line Verse	☛ Letter on how to play a game	☛ About a Place.
Game Time	☛ Picture Words	☛ Word Snake	☛ Turn Around	☛ Word Puzzle

Contents

	5 Animals	6 A Play	7 Pied Piper of Hamelin	8 A New Year's Resolution
Think	☛ Pets and Us ☛ Animal Puzzle	☛ Brain Storming on Possible Solutions	☛ Talking about Human Nature	☛ New Year Promises
Poem / Play / Story	☛ Our Little Black Dog	☛ King Barefoot Finds a Genius	☛ Pied Piper of Hamelin	☛ A New Year's Resolution
Read	☛ Rhinoceros			
Help to Understand	☛ Questions Answers	☛ Questions answers ☛ Dialogue Writing ☛ Tips for Acting	☛ Table completion ☛ Sentence completion ☛ Questions Answers	☛ Fill in the blanks ☛ Questions Answers
Useful Words	☛ Alliteration ☛ Multiple choice ☛ Antonyms		☛ Find words for given meaning	☛ Find words for given meaning ☛ Making sentences
Language in use	☛ Participles Noun Phrases		☛ Ask someone to do something	☛ Using exclamatory sentences
Before You Write	☛ Discussion on Endangered Species		☛ What goes into a Notice	☛ Listing New Year Resolutions
Now Write	☛ Rhino as an endangered species		☛ Notices	☛ New Year Resolutions
Game Time	☛ Animal Crossword		☛ Word Association	☛ Guessing Game

1 HUMAN NATURE

Think : A

Do you like packing before travelling to other places?
What do you usually carry with you?
Make a list of the things you usually carry when you travel.

_____

_____

_____

_____

_____

Read this poem about a naughty boy who thought Scotland must be a more interesting place than England.
Let us see what items the naughty boy took with him.

A Song About Myself

There was a naughty boy,
A naughty boy was he,
He would not stop at home,
He could not quiet be
He took
In his **Knapsack**,
A **Book**
Full of vowels,

And a **Shirt**
With some **Towels** –
A **slight cap**
For **night cap** –
A **Hair brush**,
Comb ditto,
New **Stockings**,
For, old ones
Would split O!

This **Knapsack**
Tight at's* back,
He riveted close
And followed his nose
To the North,
To the North,
And followed his nose
To the North!

John Keats

* at his

> **Note:**
> In reading this poem aloud stress some of the words in the middle that are capitalised, for example: Knapsack, Book, which are normally not capitalised.

Help to Understand

1. Answer the following:

a. Why is the boy described as naughty?

b. List the items that he packed in his knapsack.
   i) What book do you think he carried with him?
   ii) Why did he pack new stockings?

c. What do you think is the meaning of the following...
   Choose one of the answers:

   i) followed his nose:
   - ☐1 used a map
   - ☐2 went according to road rules
   - ☐3 went the way he felt
   - ☐4 looked at the tip of his nose

   ii) comb ditto:
   - ☐1 comb with no teeth
   - ☐2 same as above
   - ☐3 with a name on it
   - ☐4 made of ditto

   iii) riveted:
   - ☐1 fixed a door
   - ☐2 allowed it to sail
   - ☐3 fastened tight with a strap, hook or button
   - ☐4 kept it far away

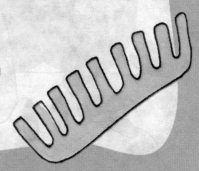

d. Rhyme

Read aloud the last words in lines:

2 and 4	8 and 10	18 and 19
5 and 7	14 and 17	20 and 21

Do you see the similarity in their sounds?
This kind of arrangement of words is called rhyme.

Work in pairs and make rhyming words:
Example: cow   try   rain   sing
              now   cry   pain   ring.

Now each pair must try and write two line poems. Put 2 or 3 words before each rhyming word and you will have your 2 line poems.

Example: Hear the fairies sing
                 Come dance in a ring.

                 Lazy boy didn't try
                 He could only cry.

Your teacher will put up your poems on the board.

Think : B

Who is a friend?
Do you have a friend?
What is it you like about your friend.

Read

A Tale of Two Friends

A potter and a washerman lived as neighbours in a city. In their youth they had been the best of friends. But now, in their later years, they had become the worst of enemies. The washerman was hardworking, and so had earned enough to feed his family well. But the potter was lazy, and he became poorer day by day.

The potter was jealous of the washerman, and wanted to see him ruined. He thought about it and came up with a plan.

Every morning the king used to go to the temple on his elephant. One morning, as the king passed by, the potter remarked, "How sad that our great king has to ride a black elephant, when it can easily be washed white."

Now the king had always wanted a white elephant. So he stopped and inquired, "My good man, I too like the idea of a white elephant. But where on earth can I find a man who can wash a black elephant white?"

"Sir, such a man lives in this very town," the potter replied. "He is a master washerman, and can wash a black elephant white by a secret process. If you send some men with me, I can take them to his house."

When the washerman saw the king's soldiers coming to his house along with the potter, he guessed that the potter was up to some mischief.

"Sir," replied the washerman bowing low, "as Your Majesty knows, to wash clothes completely white, they have to be soaked in hot water. I shall

need a pot of hot water to soak the elephant too. Please order the potter to make a pot large enough to hold the elephant."

The potter spent much time making a large pot. But the moment the elephant stepped into it, the pot broke into pieces under the elephant's weight. The potter was ordered to make stronger pots. When the potter failed to make a strong enough pot, he just ran away from the country.

Pratibha Nath and Suresh Nath

 ## Help to Understand

a. On the basis of your reading, complete the following:

1. The washerman provided his family with a good living because

   _____

2. The potter was jealous of the washerman because

   _____

3. When the king came riding on his black elephant, the potter told the king that _____

   _____

4. The king ordered the washerman to

   _____

   _____

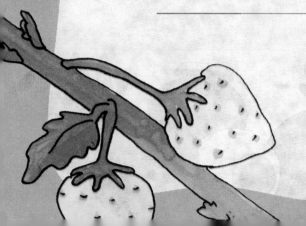

5. The king ordered the potter to _____

_____

6. The potter ran away from the country because _____

_____

b. In the table below you find the qualities of the washerman and the potter put together. Make five meaningful sentences from the table about the potter and the washerman

		Qualities
The Potter		jealous
		hardworking
	was	mischievous
		lazy
The Washerman		intelligent

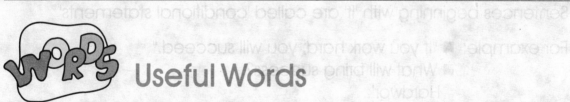 Useful Words

The meanings of some of the words from the text are given.
Find the word from the text.

meanings   words

a.   i)   a person who works with clay.   _____

     ii) a person whose occupation is
          washing clothes   _____

     iii) not friends   _____

     iv) unwilling to work   _____

     v)   destroy, spoil   _____

b. In the text you find these adjectives. Fill in the blank spaces with the comparative form of the adjectives. One has been done for you as an example :

Example: tall   **taller**

         good   _____

         bad   _____

         lazy   _____

         poor   _____

         large   _____

         strong   _____

Language in Use

Look at the following sentences:

"If you send some men with me, I can take them to his house."
"If you fail to do so, you shall be hanged."

Sentences beginning with 'If' are called 'conditional statements'

For example: ■ "If you work hard, you will succeed."
               ■ What will bring success?
                 Hardwork.
The condition for success is hardwork.

The above statement can also be rewritten as:

"If you don't work hard, you will not succeed."

Now complete the following sentences:

If you don't reach the station in time,

_____

If you respect your elders,

_____

If you cheat in the examination,

_____

Before You Write

Assume that you are studying in a boarding school and you have just returned home for a vacation. Your mother wants to know about your close friend. How will you describe him/her?

Work in groups of 4. List adjectives against each point.

Example:

appearance — tall, _____

nature — friendly, _____

likes — cricket, _____

dislikes — punishment, _____

Now Write

Write a paragraph describing your friend.

While describing remember to mention your friend's

— appearance

— nature

— likes

— dislikes

Begin

My best friend is _____

He / She is _____

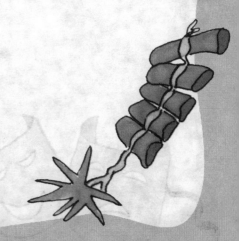

Game Time

Look at these picture words:

cl ud

br ken

pple

r pe

Now draw picture words for some of these words.

knife, snake, pencil, finger, icecream, ruler

② PEOPLE

 ## Think : A

Write down two words that come to your mind when you think of your mother.
Your teacher will list them on the blackboard.

Read

My Own Mother

She's always sewing buttons on,
Or mending things I tear;
Whenever I come home from school,
I always find her there.

She's always doing little things
That please me very much,
Like making cakes and planning trips
To parks and zoos, and such.

She's always reading stories, too,
Or teaching me a game;
And whether I've been good or bad,
She loves me just the same.

Are you surprised that I find her
Dearer than any other?
I'm sure by now you know her name,
Of course, she is my mother!

Marian Kennedy

Help to Understand

1. When does the poet mention the name of the person she is describing ? Is it at the beginning of the poem ? If you did not read the title of the poem, would you be able to guess who is described?

2. There are things that children do, all over the world. List them. Example : tear things.

3. 'Love' is a quality that all mothers have. It is also mentioned in the poem. What other qualities of a mother do you get to know from this poem?

4. Your class can now make up a poem 'Mother'. Collect the two words that each one of you thought of about your mother in the 'Think' section. Arrange them in lines and your poem is ready.

Example:

Student A   : kitchen, cooking
Student B   : loving, caring
Student C   : food, clothes
and so on.

You can end the poem with this line: "And that is Mother."

Think : B

We remember a date when it is special, like our birthday, our parents' wedding day and other birthdays in the family. There are some dates which all of us remember. Now find out what is special about the following dates :

1st	January
15th	August
14th	November
2nd	October
26th	January

This lesson is about a person who was born on the 2nd of October.

Do you know who he is?
What is his birthday known as?

 Read

Remembering Gandhiji –
A Child Like Us

In India, all children know that October 2nd is Gandhi Jayanti. It is a special birthday to remember because Mohandas Karamchand Gandhi or Mahatma Gandhi, the Father of our Nation, was a special person too. He fought against British rule but this was a fight without swords and guns. His weapons were non-violence and truth. In all the world there have been only one or two other leaders who have used those weapons. Gandhi tried to make India strong, a land of truth, love, fearlessness, brotherhood, and peace. He wanted people to give up hatred and jealousy. This great person struggled throughout his life to make Indians stop using violence and fighting over caste, language and religion. He studied the holy books of all religions and pointed out to people that all religions taught peace and brotherhood.

As a child, however, Gandhi had an upbringing just like any of us. In school, he hated games. His school taught gymnastics and cricket but he often excused himself from games. But in later life he felt sorry for not having attended games classes. The qualities, such as his great dedication to truth, were also seen to an extent in his childhood. He once secretly tried eating meat, though his family didn't approve of it. He felt very disturbed by what he had done. He imagined he

heard a goat bleat in his belly. He decided he would never touch meat again.

Once, Gandhi was tempted to smoke cigarettes, when he found his uncle smoking. But cigarettes were costly and he had no money. He stole money from his servants to buy cigarettes. But that was not enough. He picked up thrown away pieces of cigarettes from the street. His father didn't know about it. Gandhi felt guilty about his bad habit and wrote a letter to his father saying he was ready to face any punishment. His father forgave him.

In his later life too, Gandhi could look at his own faults and change himself. Once, an old woman came to him with her son and said, "My son is a diabetic, but he has a sweet tooth. I want you to advise him to stop eating sweets." Gandhi asked the woman to see him a week later. The woman returned with her son after a week. Gandhi told her son to stop eating sweets as it was bad for his condition. The woman was surprised. She wanted to know why he had not said this the previous week. Gandhi replied, "I have a sweet tooth myself. If I should advise your son, then I should stop eating sweets. I have stopped eating sweets since your last visit."

Such was his goodness. How can we live a good life? Gandhiji answers this question: "Do not lie. Keep nothing secret. Be open with your teachers and elders. Do not think of doing harm to anyone and do not talk ill of anyone. Above all, be true to yourself. That is the secret of a perfect life."

On his table he kept a toy to represent all these great thoughts. It was of three monkeys, one with palms covering the eyes, the second covering its ears and the third one with its mouth shut, to tell the world: see no evil, hear no evil and speak no evil.

Help to Understand

Answer the following questions:

1. Why is Gandhiji called the 'Father of our Nation'?

2. What weapons did he use to free India from the British?

3. What did he hate while in school? Did he feel sorry about it later? Why?

4. Why did he give up eating meat?

5. Gandhiji wrote a letter to his father about the bad habit he had picked up.
   a. What was that habit?
   b. How would you describe his action of writing to his father? For example : you could say he was truthful. What other qualities do you notice?

6. Gandhiji preached what he practised.
   This means
   a. He did not advise what he followed.
   b. He advised what he never followed.
   c. He advised what he followed.

7. There are five qualities Gandhiji felt one should have in order to lead a perfect life. What are they?

8. What do these monkeys represent?

 Useful Words

a. In the text, you find some negative and positive words. Negative words are those which give bad feelings. Positive words are those which convey good feelings. List at least five negative and positive words from the text.

positive   negative

_____   _____

_____   _____

_____   _____

b. A 'prefix' is a combination of letters placed before a word to change its meaning.

For example: 'non' placed before 'violence' becomes 'non violence', 'mis' before 'understand' becomes 'misunderstand'.
The words now have the opposite meaning.

List five more words by making use of the following prefixes:
un- in- im- dis- mis-

_____

_____

A suffix is a group of letters added at the end of a word to make another word.

For example:- 'er' placed after 'teach ' makes the word 'teacher'.
                     'or' placed after 'act' makes it 'actor'.

List at least five words for each suffix:

- ion, _____

- ness, _____

- able, _____

- ship, _____

- less, _____

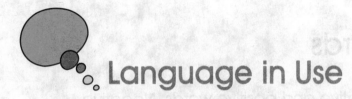

Language in Use

Look at the following expressions:

pointed out
give up
talk ill of
be true to (oneself)

Such expressions are called 'phrasal verbs'. Phrasal verbs are verbs which combine with different prepositions to make new meanings. The situation in which they are used helps us to understand them.

Fill in the blanks choosing the right phrasal verbs from the list above. Guess the meaning of the phrasal verbs as they are used in the passage:

a. To _____ your effort when you are half way through your work will be a waste of your time.

b. Tenali Rama said he wouldn't play any tricks. But he was _____ himself when he made the cat run away from the saucer of milk.

c. We should always be polite in our behaviour and speak good words. We shouldn't _____ others.

d. Piloo wrote 'April Fool' on everybody's back. But his friend _____ that he had the same on his own back.

Before You Write

In groups of four, discuss what you consider to be good habits and those that you think are bad habits. List them.

Good Habits   Bad Habits

_____   _____

_____   _____

Now Write

Now, in the same group, prepare a list of rules that you would like your class to follow, to maintain discipline. You can call it 'The Code of Conduct for Class IV'.

For example:

1. Students should maintain silence in the class when the teacher is not present.

   List some more rules in a similar manner:

   2. _____

   3. _____as_____

   4. _____

   5. _____

Game Time

You can find 15 words in this snake. The one with the most number of words is the winner.

_____

_____

_____

_____

BALLOONEARMEASUREALLYOUNGATE

3 HOBBIES

 # Think : A

What feelings come to your mind when you think of books. If you were to draw your ideas, which of these sketches would you choose?

 **Read**

Books

Books
Lead folks
To other lands.
Books
Bind folks
With friendship's bands.
Books
Tell folks
Of bygone days.
Books
Bring folks
Tomorrow's ways!

Eileen Burkard Norris

 **Help to Understand**

1. Read the poem, and answer these questions with a Yes or No.

a. Are there books that describe countries
we have not seen ? _____

b. When you want to show you are a good
friend can you give a book as a gift? _____

c. Are there books that bring people closer? _____

d. Do some books write about history? _____

e. Do some books tell us about what is going
to come in the future? _____

2. Guess the meaning of the following words. Mark (✓) against the correct meaning:

folks:	things used for eating	people	a crossing in a road
bands:	a place to keep money	a musical instrument	a ribbon to hold things together
bygone:	a snake	past	a strong wind

3. What do you notice about the last words in lines 3 and 6, 9 and 12 ?

The poet has used rhyming words.
Now make rhyming words with these.

Example:	top	bell	sum	give	mine
	pop	_____	_____	_____	_____
	mop	_____	_____	_____	_____

Think : B

Name some popular indoor and outdoor games. Which game do you like the most? Why?

Read

Chess

Chess is an indoor game which has recently become very popular. It was considered the sport of kings in olden days but now it is played by all, irrespective of whether they are young or old, male or female, strong or weak.

Chess was invented in India around the 6th century A.D. Since that time, the game has not changed much. In the 15th century, a new piece, the Queen was introduced and some minor movement adjustments were made in the 19th century.

The chess board consists of 64 white and black squares. Eight rows and eight columns make the chess board a perfect square.

There are eight pawns and eight powers consisting of one King, one Queen, two Rooks (or Castles), two Knights (or horses), two Bishops for each side. That makes 16 pieces for each side. One player plays the white pieces while the other plays black.

A person wins if he traps the opponent's King. This is called checkmate. The checkmate is a situation where a king has no place to move.

The following movements are allowed:

a. **Pawn:** moves only one step to the front. To capture the opponent's piece it can move one step across.

b. **Rook or Castle:** moves left, right, up or down any number of free squares.

c. **Bishop:** moves only diagonally any number of free squares.

d. **Knight:** moves in L shape and it is the only power which can jump over other pieces.

e. **Queen:** being the most powerful, moves left, right, up, down or diagonally any number of free squares. It combines both the powers of a Bishop and a Castle. It can travel in all eight directions.

f. King : moves only one square but in all directions. Though it can't move fast like a Queen, Castle, Knight or Bishop, the King is the head of a side. All the pawns and powers are engaged in protecting their king and aimed at trapping the opponent's King. So if the King is trapped even by a smart set of pawns or powers of the opponent, the opponent is said to be the winner. There is no use even if the trapped King has many pawns and powers left.

There are many good chess players at the international level. A young player who has earned name and fame from India is Viswanathan Anand who is presently World No. 2.

There are many tales about the game of chess. One such interesting tale is as follows:

Long back, a person who claimed that he invented this game went to a king. He explained the game to him. The king was happy and asked the person to ask for a reward. He asked for rice but he wanted each square to hold twice the number of grains than the previous one. This meant 1 grain of rice in the first square and 2 in the second, 4 in the third, 8 in the 4th and so on till all the 64 squares were filled. It seemed simple but soon the king realised it was impossible.

The grains were placed, as the man wanted. The quantity started multiplying very fast. The calculated quantity of grains for the last square was very huge, which was around 10 lakh crore tonnes (each tonne is 1000kgs). This quantity of grains can't be produced even by the entire modern world put together, for many many years.

What do you think the king did?

Help to Understand

a. Fill in the blanks:

1. The chess board consists of _____ squares.

2. A chess board has _____ rows and _____ columns.

3. When a game is about to begin, there would be _____ blank squares.

4. Each player will have _____ pieces consisting of

   pawns and _____ powers.

5. Powers include King, Queen, Rooks, and _____

6. Trapping the opponent's King is called _____

b. Match the following pieces with their movements:

Pawn — will move only diagonally.
Rook — will move in L shape.
Bishop — will move one step to the front.
Knight — will move left, right, up or down.
Queen — will move only one square in all
directions.
King — will move left, right, up, down or
diagonally.

c. Answer the following questions briefly:
i) When was chess invented ?
ii) Who played chess in the olden days?
iii) Since the day of its invention, what changes
have been made in the game of chess?
iv) In the story about chess, what did the person
ask as a reward?
v) Was it simple for the king to give the reward?
Why?

 Useful Words

a. Match the words with their correct meanings:

    words   meanings

1. popular   a. to catch or trap, obtain by force
2. irrespective   b. to make known to others
3. invent   c. happening in turns, first the one and then the other
4. introduce   d. liked by a lot of people
5. alternatively   e. accepted as a fact, understood
6. columns   f. not taking something into account
7. capture   g. big
8. diagonal   h. vertical section
9. huge   i. number of things in a line
10. realised   j. to make something that didn't exist before

b. Homophones:

Homophones are words which are pronounced in the same way but are spelt differently.

For example: son / sun   our / hour   flu / flew
sent / scent   waist / waste

Write a homophone in the space provided, taking help from the hints given in the brackets:

i. tire / _____ [rubber filled with air used in vehicles]

ii. pray / _____ [an animal that is killed by another for food]

iii. sale / _____ [to travel by ship]

iv. fare / _____ [good in colour]

v. wait / _____ [mass of an object]

vi. right / _____ [use a pen , pencil or chalk]

Language in Use

To express ourselves, we use either polite forms or give instructions. Sentences making requests and giving instructions are called imperative sentences.

Request: There are various ways of making a request, for example:
1. Please bring me a glass of water.
2. Could you lend me your bicycle for four days?
3. May I have your book?
4. Shall we go to the zoo today?

Now, make four sentences using various forms of request. Follow the examples.

_____

_____

_____

Instruction : When you want someone to do something, you give instructions. For example, when you give your friend directions to reach the stadium, you will say:

1. Go straight.
2. Turn to the left.
3. Take the first right turn.

Now, give instructions to your friend on how to play carrom.

Before You Write

Here is a new game of Noughts and Crosses.
This game is played by two players. 100 squares are drawn on a piece of paper i.e. 10 Squares across and 10 squares down. The players have to decide who will draw noughts and who will draw crosses.

Each player, in turn, draws a nought or a cross in one of the squares. To win the game, one must have atleast five noughts or crosses in a row vertically, horizontally or diagonally. The opponent moves in such a way that the other cannot draw noughts or crosses in a row.

Discuss the following points about the game with your partner.

a. number of players

b. material required

c. who is the winner?

d. fun of the game

e. what does the game require from the players?

Now Write

Write a letter to your pen friend in the USA. Give a brief description of the game Noughts and Crosses in your letter. Include the points you discussed. Do not forget to write your address and the date in the letter at the appropriate place.

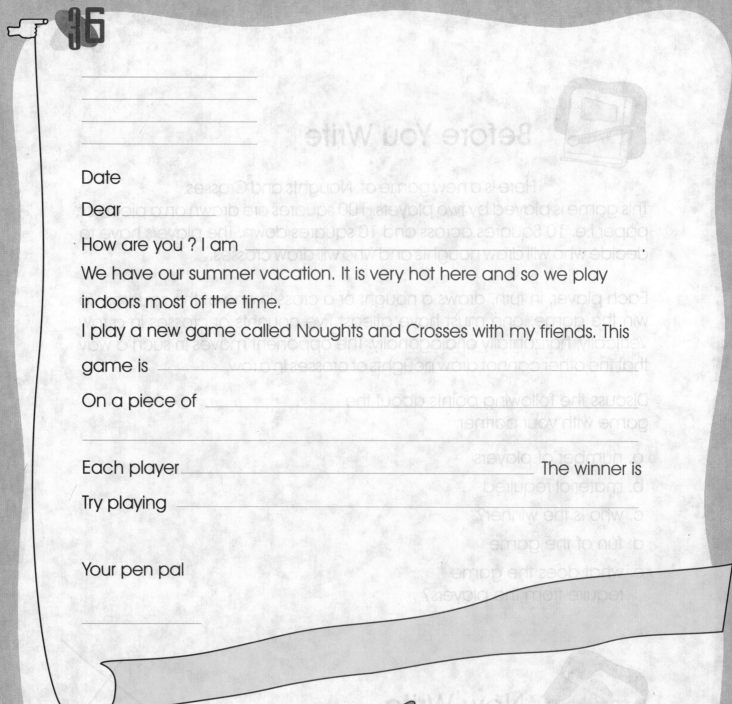

_____
_____
_____

Date
Dear _____
How are you ? I am _____
We have our summer vacation. It is very hot here and so we play
indoors most of the time.
I play a new game called Noughts and Crosses with my friends. This
game is _____
On a piece of _____
_____
Each player _____ The winner is
Try playing _____

Your pen pal

_____

Game Time
Turn Around.

Tap is a word whose letters can be shuffled around to make PAT. Think of more
such words which can be rearranged to get a new word. Write them down.

_____

_____

④ ENVIRONMENT

Think : A

Imagine a world without trees.
Work in groups of 3.
List 3 things that you would not
have if there were no trees.

Read

My Tree

O Tree, so big and stout and strong,
You've lived so very, very long;
A hundred years or more I'm told,
And yet you're not so very old.

A hundred secrets you could tell,
Of children whom you love so well,
Who came and sat beneath your shade,
Or underneath your branches played.

A hundred birds have built their nests,
Your leaves have softly kissed their breasts,
Your branches seem to touch the sky;
Yet you were once as small as I.

Someday when I have grown up too,
I'm coming back to visit you;
And changed though other things will be,
I'll find the same dear friendly tree.

Garnet Engle

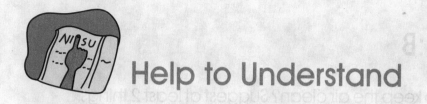

Help to Understand

a. Complete these sentences:

1. The age of the tree must be _____
2. The tree must have helped lots of _____ and _____
3. A hundred years is a long time for a ____ but not for a _____

b. Answer the following questions:

1. How do we know that the tree loves children and birds? How does it help them?
2. The tree is described just as a friend is described. What would the child share with the tree? What would the child want to do when he grows up?
3. What does the tree do to visitors to show its love and care?
4. You learned about rhyme in an earlier poem. How many sets of words rhyme in this poem?
5. The tree is described like a person. This is usually done in poetry. An angry man can be described as 'the blazing sun'.

Now match the persons in column B with the qualities in column A :

A	B
blazing sun	the king
shy fox	a woman with flowing hair
proud lion	a wise person
a waterfall	cunning person
an owl	angry person
the earth	a patient mother

 ## Think :B

What can we all do to keep the air clean? Suggest at least 2 things.

_____

What should we not do in order not to pollute the air? Suggest 2 things.

_____

 Read the story of Uncle Randy's invention to find out:

Stop the Smoke, Please !
We Want to Live.

Uncle Randy said he was an inventor. Pete was always curious to see what he invented in that brick shed with a tin roof, in a corner of the garden, with the chimney belching smoke. Mom said Pete was not to go in there. The smells were bad to inhale. There were vapours, smoke puffing out of all kinds of pots and pans and the chiddlinck-chiddlinck of some engine making a constant racket.

The neighbours complained. But Uncle Randy wouldn't listen. He always boasted the world would some day come to know what a great inventor

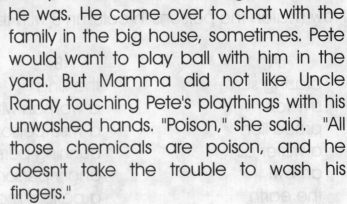

he was. He came over to chat with the family in the big house, sometimes. Pete would want to play ball with him in the yard. But Mamma did not like Uncle Randy touching Pete's playthings with his unwashed hands. "Poison," she said. "All those chemicals are poison, and he doesn't take the trouble to wash his fingers."

And it came out one day – Uncle Randy's invention – a single-seat cart on three wheels with a pipe leading upwards and one pointing behind.

Everyone came rushing out of the house the morning they heard this tremendous racket – chidddr, chidddr,.... rrr rr .. Even Father, who always thought Uncle Randy cranky and a nuisance, came out to see. The great invention was rolled out of the shed first with a wobble; then something went whirr.. between the wheels and set the engine working. The chiddr became a loud sputter. Uncle Randy sitting proudly atop the vehicle as though he were on a royal throne, pressed a kind of pump at his foot and the vehicle moved forward with a louder sputter.

But goodness! What was this? A cloud of black smoke puffed out of the pipes at either end and rings and more clouds of black smoke came out. Uncle Randy circled the yard once and suddenly shut down the engine, and letting the vehicle fall to a side, jumped off it and collapsed into a chair in a fit of coughing. Everyone quickly covered their nostrils with handkerchiefs, including Mamma, who quickly ran into the kitchen and brought him a hot cup of tea to stop the cough.

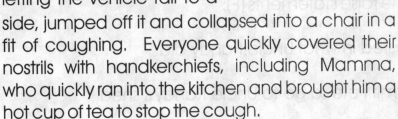
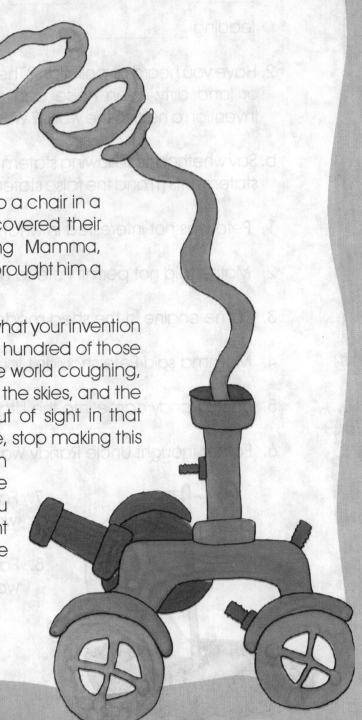

"Thank God," said Father, "we know what your invention can do to the world. If you made a hundred of those horrible machines, they will set all the world coughing, until it rocks the earth off its course in the skies, and the Sun, the Moon, everything goes out of sight in that frightful cloud of smoke. Listen to me, stop making this smoking monster. There are enough inventors in the world to make smokefree vehicles. So, don't you meddle in serious matters. Plant some good trees, instead. They'll take care of the world's health."

Uncle Randy managed a weak shamefaced smile.

Help to Understand

a. Complete the sentences by filling in the blanks:

1. Uncle Randy was trying to make a _____ with three _____ and a
   _____ on top. It had _____ one leading _____ and one
   leading _____.

2. Have you heard of 'pollution'? The word means: making the air or water
   or land dirty. Even noise can cause pollution. Was Uncle Randy's
   invention a help to the world? Why do you think so?

b. Say whether the following statements are true or false. Mark the true
   statements (T) and the false statements (F).

1. Pete was not interested in what Uncle Randy did.

2. Mother did not permit Pete to go to Uncle Randy's shed.

3. Some engine in the shed made noise sometimes.

4. Mamma said Pete shouldn't touch his playthings.

5. Uncle Randy came into the kitchen for tea.

6. Father thought Uncle Randy was a bothersome madman.

7. Father thought the sun and the moon would be frightened.

8. Father said trees are good for the world.

Useful Words

a. Match the words in column A with their meaning in column B.

A	B
inventor	to breathe in
belching	tiny drops of water in the air which appear like smoke
inhale	loud unpleasant noise
vapours	liquids, powders or gas (made in a laboratory)
pans	move unsteadily from side to side
racket	giving out large amounts of (smoke, steam or fire)
chemicals	the first person to make or use a machine
wobble	containers with long handles
collapsed	did something with difficulty
managed	suddenly fell down

b. How many words expressing sounds can you find in this story?
   Example: Chiddlinck - Chiddlinck

_____

_____

Name words that express the following sounds.
Their first letters are given:

1. speaking into somebody's ear   w _ _ _ _ _ _ _

2. the sound of a big bell   d _ _ _ _ d _ _ _

3. the sound of tiny silver bells   t _ n k _ _ _

4. beating on a tin with a stick   t _ _ _ _ _ _ _

5. burst of a cracker   b _ _ _ _

Language in Use

Mark (✓) against the correct meaning of the underlined words.

He was sitting proudly <u>as though</u> he were on a royal throne

    1. above
    2. like
    3. straight

Smoke puffed out of the pipes <u>at either end</u>

    1. one end
    2. one end and the other
    3. no end

<u>Rock</u> the earth <u>off its course</u>

    1. shake it to change its direction
    2. swing it gently
    3. keep the earth in its path

Everything <u>goes out of sight</u>

    1. becomes blind
    2. is not to be seen
    3. goes out of control

They'll <u>take care of</u> the world's health

    1. trouble
    2. look after
    3. take out

Inventors make <u>smoke free</u> vehicles

    1. without smoke
    2. giving smoke without payment
    3. with extra smoke

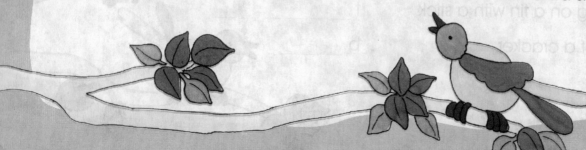

Uncle Randy managed a <u>shamefaced</u> smile

1. a face with a smile
2. a face expressing shame
3. a face like that of shame

Before You Write

Put down some points before you go on to describe a beautiful natural setting like a hillstation / seaside / or riverside/ or jungle area / or even a beautiful place you have seen on the TV.

You will find the following phrases useful. They will make your writing more interesting.

It is a place which _____

Its greatest attraction is _____

_____

What makes it special is _____

You would love to _____

Of all the places I've seen, this is the best _____

It is also necessary to add adjectives to any description. Choose some from the following when you write your description. You may also add your own.

colourful, cool,
pleasant wonderful, peaceful, unpolluted
smokefree, breezy, clean

Now Write

Write a paragraph about a beautiful place, you would like to visit. Do not forget to describe the place. Use adjectives that will make your description interesting.

_____

_____

_____

_____

Game Time

Here are some 3 letter words. Their spelling is jumbled up.
Rewrite them correctly in the spaces next to each.

TEW ___ ◯ ___

APC ___ ◯ ___

YRT ___ ___ ◯

ELD ___ ◯ ___

CRA ___ ___ ◯

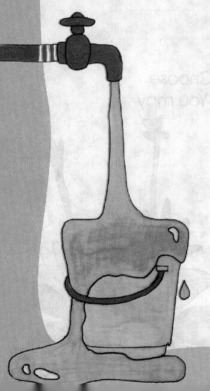

⇐ Here's a picture

Use the letters in the circles and find
the answer tothe riddle:

Don't waste this _ _ _ _ _ _

5 ANIMALS

Think : A

How many of you keep pet
animals at home?
Are they like us sometimes? Stubborn?
Eager to eat? Play?
Do what they like?

Here's one very much like us. She won't do what she is expected to do.

 Read

Our Little Black Dog

Our little black dog barks at each tiny thing –
A fly on a fence or a bird on the wing,
A leaf on a tree or a kite in the sky,
A crumpled-up newspaper scurrying by,
She grumbles at gravel and pebbles and stones;
She bellows at branches and dirty old bones;
She trumpets at insects – a beetle or bee,
But – bark at a stranger? No, not she!

We wanted a watchdog, and that's what we got –
Except that she watches the thing she should not!
Good leather shoes that are easy to chew,
Soft comfy cushions, so fluffy and new,
She watches for letters and papers and books;
She watches for food scraps each time Mother cooks;
She watches for offers to sit on a knee,
But – watch for a stranger? No, not she!

Daphne Doward

Help to Understand

1. Does the little black dog keep watch well?

   Is your answer: Yes, definitely
   No, definitely not, or
   Yes, but _____?

   Tick the right answer.

2. What does she like to _____ .

   chew on   a._____   b._____

   tear up   a._____   b._____   c._____

   eat   a._____

   rest on   a._____

3. a. Find all the sounds that the dog makes

   a._____   b._____   c._____   d._____

   Add 2 more starting with g _____ and s _____

   b. List the sounds that some other creatures make, such as:

   owl   : _____

   cat   : _____

   tiger : _____

   cuckoo : _____

4. If you look at the poem carefully, you will find at least two words starting with the same letter in each line.

Example : Line 1– black, barks

Line 2 – fly, fence

Try to make such word groups. See that when you put two words beginning with the same sounds the words go together and make sense.

Example: calm cow, black bull, fly far away

_____

_____

Think : B

Look at the pictures given above. Can you recognize these animals. Unscramble the letters given below to find out their names.

(I)   RUTLET _____

(II) NLOI _____

(III) GRTEI _____

(IV) LIRALOG _____

(V) DCLOERIOC _____

(VI) CENHIORSOR _____

What do the above animals have in common? They are all wild animals who live in the jungle. Now read about one of them, the rhinoceros, in the text given below.

 # Read

Rhinoceros

In the prehistoric age, many strange and huge animals roamed the land. Almost all those animals ceased to exist long ago. The rhinoceros managed to survive. So it is still around.

The rhino is in no way a pleasant looking beast. It has a large and massive body with stout, powerful legs and thick skin. It has a horn (sometimes two) on the snout (nose). The horn is not really a horn or a bone, but tufts of hair plastered together to form a hard growth. If broken off, another grows in its place. The horn is used as a weapon by the rhino to protect itself. The rhino's mouth is rather small. Its ear is shaped like a cornet, with hair along the edges. Its tail is short with hair on the lower part. The hard skin of the rhino is in reality, quite soft. It can be cut even with a small knife. When dry, the skin gets hardened.

There are five kinds of rhinos in the world. In size, the Indian rhino is second only to the white one of Africa. The Indian rhino has only one horn. Both the male and the female rhinos have horns of the same size. The skin is very thick and lies in folds around the body and on the shoulder. They eat grass and reed.

The Indian rhino is about 180 cms high at the shoulder. The animal lives a solitary life as a rule. Several may occupy the same jungle, each having its own patch. Because of weak eyesight, it cannot see much on either side. Therefore, when it attacks an object, it charges in a straight line. All that has to be done to avoid the charge is to step to one side as the animal approaches.

Rhinos were found in large numbers in India from the prehistoric period. From the north west frontier region to Assam, the animal was widely distributed in the jungles at the foot of the Himalayan ranges and also in the forests below the Gangetic valley. As time passed, the population of the rhinos became small and in many areas in India, they have become extinct. Now, rhinos are found only in Assam, Bengal and the lower parts of Nepal.

The rhino horn has medicinal properties. It fetches a high price today. For this reason, people kill a large number of rhinos. This is one of the causes for the fall in the rhino population. In some places, even the blood and the urine of the rhino are valued as medicines.

In India, the rhinoceros is protected by law. No one is allowed to kill the animal. Yet illegal killing of the animal continues.

The Kaziranga wild life sanctuary has been established in Assam for preservation of the rhinos. There are many rhinos in the sanctuary and it is hoped that there the animals will have a better chance of survival.

From 'Animal World', a CBT publication.

Help to Understand

1. Below you see a table with various columns. From the text, fill in important informations about the rhinoceros.

Age to which it belongs	Physical appearance and height	Special features	Food	Places where it is found

2. Answer the following questions:

a. What is special about the rhino's skin?
b. Why does the animal attack in a straight line?
c. What are the reasons for the fall in rhino population?
d. How is the animal protected in India? What are the measures taken for its preservation?

Useful Words

1. Below are listed a few words with three meanings given for each word. Choose the meaning which is nearest to the given word.

For example : roam : a. move
b. wander around
c. walk
The meaning of roam is wander around

a. prehistoric :   a. of the ancient period
b. out of date
c. modern

b. massive:
  a. huge
  b. light
  c. heavy

c. snout:
  a. head
  b. jaws
  c. an animal's long projecting nose

d. cornet:
  a. musical instrument like a small trumpet
  b. cone-shaped
  c. a cone-shaped wafer holding icecream

e. extinct :
  a. decline
  b. no longer active
  c. no longer existing in living form.

f. miraculous:
  a. related to supernatural elements
  b. remarkable
  c. wonderful

g. illegal:
  a. based on law
  b. against the law
  c. to make money

b. Antonyms are words that are opposite in meaning.
   Give antonyms for the following:

a. intelligent _____

b. black _____

c. courageous _____

d. fast _____

e. hot _____

f. sharp _____

g. thick _____

h. big _____

i. long _____

j. hard _____

k. beautiful _____

l. winner _____

Language in Use

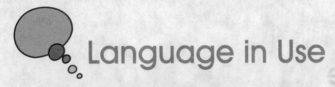

Species that are in danger can be called 'endangered species'
Now, how will you say the following ?

1. a surface that is polished _____
2. a light that is dazzling _____
3. a corner of the garden that is shady _____
4. a man with broad shoulders _____
5. a cricketer who is left handed _____
6. a lady with blue eyes _____
7. a shirt with an open neck _____

Before You Write

Some animals have become extinct i.e. they exist no more.
Some animals are in the process of becoming extinct. They are
called endangered species.

Discuss in groups of four, the following questions. Write down the points
i. Why are animals killed by man ?
ii. Which animals are being killed in large numbers and why ?
iii. What should be our role in protecting such animals ?

Now Write

'The Rhino is in danger of extinction'.
Write two paragraphs :
Why is the rhino endangered ?
What is the government doing
to protect the rhino?

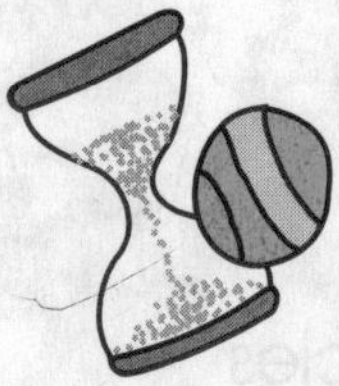

Game Time

Complete this animal puzzle. The clues will help you.

Clues

Down

1. running in races (5)
2. a large animal with a tusk and a trunk (8)
3. wicked and cruel (4)
5. pet, loving and loyal domestic animal (3)
6. a wild bull (2)
8. in cricket, you cannot hit the ball without this (3)

Across

1. rabbit like animal (4)
4. king of the forest (4)
5. gentle but fast running animal (4)
7. known for its cunning (3)
8. nick named Teddy (4)
9. feared most by rats (3)
10. India's national animal (5)

6 KING BAREFOOT FINDS A GENIUS

Think

Ask your friends these questions:
You have only 3 days left for an examination and you aren't prepared.
How do you handle the problem?

a. How many of you tell everyone you are sick?
b. How many of you think it is better to copy from
   somebody else?
c. How many of you think of running away somewhere?
d. How many of you decide to make the best use of time
   and prepare intelligently?

Here is a play of a kingdom where everyone went barefoot. It is a
story of a long, long time ago before a useful invention was made.

Read
King Barefoot Finds a Genius

Characters:

King Barefoot of Thornbushland

Chief Minister Kindasmart

Minister Greedenvy

Minister Wilyglee

Guard One

Guard Two

Scene I :

Guard One : Hello friend, do you know if the King is going for a walk?

Guard Two : I hope not. He would want to go round Eastside of Thornbushland.

Guard One : Why do you say that?

Guard Two : This is a peculiar land. Thorns, thorns, everywhere! So much thorn and the King must walk! Why can't he ride in his chariot and let us poor folks take the thorns into our feet?

Guard One : Why are you afraid of his going to Eastside?

Guard Two : Ooh, the men had to clear the ground of thorns and bushes when he took a walk on Westside, Southside and Northside, and the wretched bushes grew back in two days flat. And they all grumbled about it for days together. Their shoulders ached, they said.

Guard One : And isn't Eastside cleared of thorns and bushes?

Guard Two : No. Not yet. The men's fingers are all still sore from chopping bushes and lifting bundles of thorny branches. So they have all taken the day off.

Guard One : Ah, I hear the sound of the chariot. It must be the King and his ministers. Ouch! a thorn in my foot. Let us move out of the way first, ah....ooh......

Scene II:

King Barefoot : It is a fine day. And I'm in the mood for a walk on Eastside.

Chief Minister : Oh, but, Your Majesty ....er..... could I make a suggestion? You could travel by chariot and we'll all follow on foot. That way, you could see the whole of Eastside and much faster too.

King Barefoot : No, Chief Minister. I wish to walk. Don't stop me.

Chief Minister : I wouldn't want to go against your wish, Your Majesty. But still the King is the King, ... and to walk among common people ....

King Barefoot : I say, don't stop me. You impertinent fool! (he jumps off the chariot and immediately screams in pain) Aah! terrible! a thousand curses. What is this vicious weapon that has stuck into my foot?

Who is the wicked enemy who has laid it in my path? Ooh! Aah! ... (hobbles on one foot and hops back into the chariot. The minister quickly rushes and pulls out the thorn. Tears a piece of his vest and binds the King's foot.)

Chief Minister : Oh, pardon me, pardon me, Your Majesty. Those are not the weapons of the enemy. Those are thorns from the thornbush.

King Barefoot : (angrily) Thornbush? What is a thornbush? What is it doing in my beautiful land? Ooh... aah...

Chief Minister : It isn't .... isn't...a .. a.. thornbush, Your Majesty. Our beautiful land is full of them .... As its name shows.

King Barefoot : What?....and you didn't even tell me about it all these years? Off with every thornbush before the week is out.

Chief Minister : But, Your Majesty, you must forgive me. Honestly, if I may remind you, your great grandfather imported the thornbush specially from Saudi Arabia and tended to it with great care.... and now the thornbush refuses to leave our beautiful land. It's not my...

King Barefoot : Don't say a word more. Or I'll have your head chopped off (still wincing in pain).... Ah! I know – you say it is my great grandfather's special gift to our land. We'll keep every thornbush in the land. But you, if you want to keep your head in its place and keep your job too, you had better see that wherever I step in my kingdom, that place is covered in leather in exactly a month from now so that I can walk down any street I wish.

Chief Minister (in alarm) : But Your Majesty, that will mean killing all the cattle for leather, instead of cutting down the thornbush.

King Barefoot : Silence! I shall get back to the Palace now. Remember only one month.

King goes away. Chief Minister sits on a stone bench with his face in his palms, worried how to pave the entire kingdom with leather in one month.

(Wilyglee and Greedenvy watch from a distance)

Wilyglee : One month! This rogue is finished.

Greedenvy : Paving the whole kingdom with leather! ..He'll kill all the cattle. There'll be no milk and no animal to work the farms a nd fields... and still there won't be enough leather to cover the whole kingdom. Ha ha! Let us watch his head roll.

Wilyglee : Then, of course, the King will have to appoint a new Chief Minister. I wonder who that will be!

Greedenvy : Of course! He'll again order the new CM to pave the entire kingdom with leather, and one more head will roll.

Wilyglee : Now, we can wait for one month and watch the first head roll. And then, maybe the King will change his mind.

Greedenvy : I hope the King doesn't change his mind before the end of the month.

Scene III:

One month later.

Guard : Today is the day. Nothing has been done to pave the kingdom with leather. The King looks very angry and the CM is so nervous.

King Barefoot : What do you have to say, Chief Minister, now that the month is over? How do you save my noble feet from thorns? I am ready to take a walk on Northside, Westside, Southside and Eastside right away.

Wilyglee and Greedenvy : (Whispering) the rogue is properly trapped! He has not moved even a pin in this last month!

Chief Minister : Ready, Your Majesty.

King Barefoot : What! Do you mean there is leather under foot everywhere?

Chief Minister : Yes indeed, Your Majesty. Your humble servant... (Bends towards the King's feet)

King Barefoot : You dishonest fellow! Don't expect a pardon by falling at my feet.

Chief Minister : I wish to touch your feet, Your Majesty, before you decide.

King Barefoot : Okay. One last time.

(Wilyglee and Greedenvy laugh in their sleeves and exchange eager glances)

Chief Minister : (bends and puts a pair of leather shoes on the King's feet) Now, Your Majesty, there'll be leather wherever you step In your kingdom.

King Barefoot : You are a genius! You shall own Half of Eastside as a reward!

(Wilyglee and Greedenvy faint)

Help to Understand

1. Why did the King call the Chief Minister a 'genius' ?
   In what way was the King the opposite of the Chief Minister ?

   a. What the King didn't know: _____

   b. What the Chief Minister knew: _____

2. Do you think the King's stupidity ran in his family? Pick out a sentence from the story to move this.

3. What kind of work did the ordinary people of Thornbushland do?

4. When they saw the Chief Minister rewarded for his brilliant idea, Wilyglee and Greedenvy fainted. What do you think they would have said to one another afterwards? Fill in the lines below to make a dialogue:

   Wilyglee : I feel so disappointed ! I was hoping that _____

   _____

   Greedenvy: I knew it would be difficult for anybody to fulfil the King's

   orders. But I never thought that the Chief Minister would _____

   _____

5. The King makes a proclamation (a public announcement) that he is rewarding the Chief Minister. Write it as he must have done it. Start as given below :

   'The King of Thornbushland announces a reward of half of Eastside to the Chief Minister. The Chief Minister has made an important invention called shoes

   _____ One day, _____

   _____

(Please remember that the King is making this proclamation. So he certainly won't say that he was angry and foolish). Announce this proclamation in class.

1. Acting the play.

   Now that you have read this play, you may want to act it. Work in groups of 4. Let us think of all that we need to act the play within the classroom. We need not use curtains and costumes as in a stage drama but we can still make it appear real. For example, we can choose a tall or heavy person to play the king.

- How many more people do you need?
- Should they look bright, lean, pretty, serious, funny?
- Remember, we are only trying to act. So a person who can make his face look wicked is not really wicked by nature.
  So what kind of face should each actor make?
- What items in the classroom / school can be used to mean something in the play?
  For example: A chair can be the chariot. What about a crown, sword and such things ?
- What about actions?
  At what point in the story will people talk in whispers, like exchanging a secret?
  When will they lean forward to see what is happening?
  When will they stand with arms folded and head bowed?
  When will they limp and fold a foot by the hand?
  When will they walk proudly?

2. Now, the groups can tell the rest of the class their answers and agree on the best answers.

   Select people from the class to act each part. Your teacher will now divide the class into 5 groups. Each group will prepare one actor (one group will prepare the two guards)
   Now act the play in front of the class. You need not learn the lines by heart. Everyone can read out of the book while acting. But practise reading in advance.

7 THE PIED PIPER OF HAMELIN

 **Think**

The words listed describe human nature. What do they suggest?

Example:

generous   A person who cares and helps the needy

cheat   _____

friendly   _____

cunning   _____

revengeful   _____

Now read the story to see if there are any characters in the story who fit your description.

Read
The Pied Piper of Hamelin Town

About the story:

This legend dates from the thirteenth or fourteenth century and has many variations. The poem by Robert Browning is perhaps the best known and is presented here in a short story form.

Vocabulary and pronunciation guide:

Hamelin [HAM-lin]
guilders [GILL-durs] : a unit of money in old Germany; like a dollar

1. Once a long, long time ago, in Germany in a region called Brunswick, there was a pleasant town known as Hamelin. But the houses were full of rats. They were everywhere.

> Rats!
> They fought the dogs and killed the cats,
> And bit the babies in the cradles,
> And ate the cheeses out of the vats,
> And licked the soup from the cooks' own ladles.

2. At last it got so bad that the people simply couldn't stand it any longer, and so they all gathered at the town hall and demanded that the Mayor and the city council of Hamelin town put an end to these rats at once.

3. Well, the poor Mayor didn't know what to do. He sat in his office with his head in his hands, and he thought, and thought, and thought.

Suddenly there came a little tap-tap at his door. And in came the strangest figure! He wore a long coat that was half yellow and half red. And round his neck he had a long red and yellow ribbon, and on it hung a flute, or something like a flute anyway, and his fingers went up and down it as if he wanted to be playing.

4. He approached the Mayor and said, "If you'd like to get rid of the rats I can do it for you."

"You can?" cried the Mayor. "How? Who are you, anyway?"

"I am known as the Pied Piper," said the man, "and I have a way to draw after me everything that walks or flies or swims. Will you give me a thousand guilders if I rid your town of rats?"

"A thousand?" exclaimed the Mayor. "Why, I'll give you fifty thousand guilders. But I don't believe you can."

"All right," said the Piper, "it is a bargain."

And then he went to the door and stepped out into the street and he put his musical pipe to his lips and began to play a strange, high, little tune.

Three shrill notes the pipe uttered,

You heard as if an army muttered;

And the muttering grew to a grumbling;

And the grumbling grew to a mighty rumbling;

And out of the houses the rats came tumbling!

Great rats, small rats, lean rats, brawny rats,

Brown rats, black rats, gray rats, tawny rats,

Grave old plodders, gay young friskers,

Fathers, mothers, uncles, cousins,

Cocking tails and pricking whiskers,

Families by tens and dozens,

Brothers, sisters, husbands, wives-

Followed the Piper for their lives!

5. From street to street he piped, and they followed, dancing, till they came down to the edge of the big river, and there the Piper turned sharply about and stepped aside, and all those rats tumbled hurry-scurry, head over heels, down the bank into the river and were drowned.

6. The people, old and young alike, waved their hats and jumped up and down with glee.

7. The Piper now asked for his thousand guilders.

"Hm-er-a thousand guilders" said the Mayor. "Of course that was all a joke, don't you see?"

"I do not joke," said the Piper in a quiet but stern manner. "Give me a thousand guilders now, if you please."

"Oh, come now," said the Mayor. "Here, take fifty guilders and go away."

"Will you give me my thousand guilders or not?" said the Piper.

The Mayor said "No."

Then the Piper warned the Mayor very softly, "I know another tune than that which I played. I play it to those who cheat me."

"Play what you please!" replied the Mayor. "You can't frighten me! Go ahead, do your worst!"

8. Once more the Piper stepped into the street, and began to play a little tune, soft and sweet and very, very strange. And before he played three little notes, all the children came running out of the houses to follow him.

"Stop, stop!" cried the people. "He is taking our children! Stop him, Mayor!"

"I will give you your money. I promise I will!" cried the Mayor, and he tried to run after the Piper.

9. But the music made the children dance and the grown-ups stand stock-still. There they stood and saw the Piper playing his little tune, with the children dancing at his heels. Till he came to the bank of the river.

10. "Oh, no!" the people cried, "he's going to drown our children in the river!" But the Piper turned and went along by the riverbank, and all the children followed after. Up, and up, and up a hill toward a mountain. Suddenly, the mountainside opened - just like two great doors, and the Piper went through the opening, with all the children and just as they got through, the great doors closed.

11. One little lame child, who couldn't keep up with the rest didn't get there in time.

adapted from the poem by **Robert Browning**

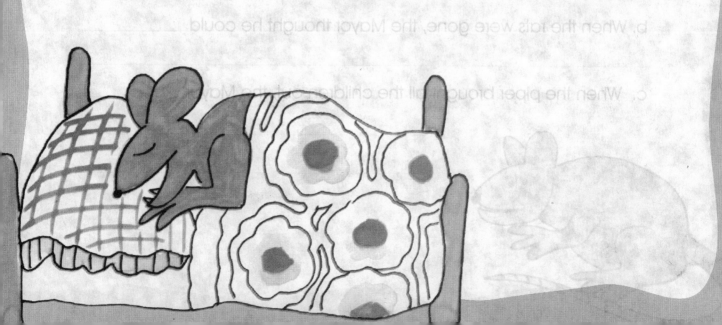

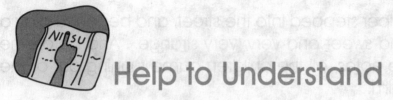

Help to Understand

1. This story has some repeated actions but with changes. Fill in the blanks to show the changes between the first time and the second time

	1st time	2nd time
a. The mayor promises	fifty thousand guilders	_____ guilders
b. The piper's tune is	_____	soft, sweet and _____
c. The piper was followed by	_____	
d. When the rats were gone, the Mayor thought	the piper couldn't frighten him.	he _____

2. Complete the following sentences:

a. Before the piper came the Mayor didn't know _____

_____

b. When the rats were gone, the Mayor thought he could _____

_____

c. When the piper brought all the children out, the Mayor _____

_____

_____

3. Why didn't the people stop the piper from taking away their children?

_____

_____

4. What is the lesson the Mayor learned? Did the people of the town learn a lesson too?

_____

_____

Do you think the Mayor deserved the punishment? Work with a partner and decide what punishment you would give him.

_____

_____

Help to Understand

1. You have a description of the rats of Hamelin town. If rats are allowed to grow in large numbers what will happen to a town? Read the verses again.

2. Comprehension.
   Complete these statements:

The rats were unafraid of _____ , _____ , and people.

They were terrible because they _____ babies, the _____ ,

_____ the cats, and no _____ was safe.

3. Did the rats come with one great noise (as when school gives over and all the children yell) or did the noise grow bigger and bigger as more of them came out? Write the lines that give you the answer.

Say the words muttering, grumbling and rumbling with the sound rising. Which of these sounds is small and rather hard to hear?

4. The words cradles, vats and ladles appear almost at the beginning of the story. Identify these objects from the pictures given below, and write the name of the object beneath each picture.

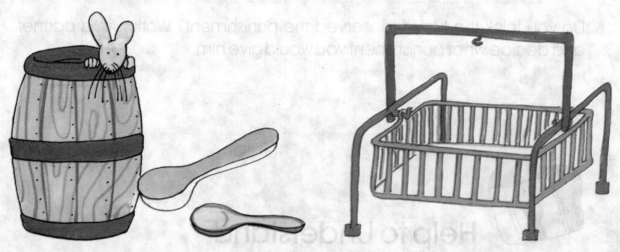

Useful Words

a. Match the following words with their meaning:

plodders   pointing sharply

friskers   lifting and turning in some direction

cocking   those who move slowly

pricking   those that move and jump and run about

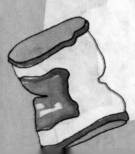

b. Word puzzle:

There are some words in the story, whose meanings are given. Identify these words from the meanings and paragraph number given in brackets. Some clues to the spelling are also given:

a. Made a firm request (2) __ e __ a __ __ e __

b. An agreement to pay (4) __ a __ __ __ a i __

c. Died by going under water (5) __ __ o __ __ e __

d. An area of land that is higher than the land around it (10) __ i __ __

e. A bigger and higher hill with steep sides (10) __ o u __ __ a i __

f. Gave a new name to (11) __ e __ a __ e __

Language in Use

Want someone to do something?
How do you ask?
Look at the example.

Can you bandage my finger?

The patient wants the nurse to bandage his finger.
There are various ways of asking.

Look at what these people are doing and match the speech bubbles to the correct pictures by writing the corresponding numbers next to them.

1. Please listen.

2. Could you give me direction ?

3. Can you repair the tap ?

5. Could you pass the spoon, please ?

4. Would you take our photograph ?

Before You Write

a. When something is missing you can put up a notice describing it and offer a reward to the finder.

Let us look at some examples:

The people of Hamelin put up notices outside their doors when the rats carried away things. Some of them are given here:

Missing **5th May**

An orange pencil box with pencils and eraser was lost in the classroom yesterday. The name Kohl is engraved on the top. Good reward will be given.

Return to Anna
5, Mona Lane

Missing **3rd June**

One gold earring with two red stones is missing. It was lost in the playground last evening. The finder will be rewarded.

Return it to Hans
25, Salt Street

Missing **9th Dec**

A white, silver baby's porridge bowl has been missing for two days. The letters BL are written on it. Reward will be offered to the finder.

Return it to Leda
3, Burgen Street

Now read the notices given above and fill in the these columns.

Details	Object 1	Object 2	Object 3
1. What		earring	
2. Where			classroom
3. When			
4. Other details			silver
5. Reward offered			
6. Names and address		Leda	

b. You can also write a notice about an event, if you want to invite everybody to it. Example:

Notice
**Drama by Class IV will
be at 2 o' clock on 16.9.99
in the Auditorium.
Only 50 seats are available.**

**Give your names to
Alka, class leader of IV C.**

Notice
**Sports selection of
Tagore House will be held
at 3.00 p.m. on 15th March
in the Playground.**

**All those who want to join
the skipping race should
meet Raja, House Leader
of Tagore House.**

Now write down the details given in these notices.

Details	Event 1	Event 2
1.		
2.		
3.		
4.		
5.		

Now Write

Now write a notice for each of the following:
a. a lunch box lost in the school
b. a fancy dress competition conducted by class IV

Do not forget to include all the details.

Game Time

How many words of description can you use for children? Try and list them.

Example: small boys, pretty girls, naughty children .... quiet children

For flowers in a garden?

For the toys in a toy shop?

For the animals in the zoo?

8 A NEW YEAR'S RESOLUTION

 ## Think

Do you make promises to change
or give up old habits when a New Year begins?
How many promises have you kept so far?

Let us see what happened to a spider and a fly. Read this story to find out why they promised to change.

Read

A New Year's Resolution

1. On a morning of a New Year's day, a spider caught a fly in her web and was just going to eat him up for lunch, when a woman with a broom swept the spider, the fly, the cobweb and all into a dustbin.

2. The spider pulled her legs in tight so as not to lose the ant. She was tossed about in the dust. At last she reached a place where all was dark and soft and dusty. The spider looked with all her eight eyes, but she could not see a single thing. She couldn't think what had happened.

3. At last the woman put a lid on the dustbin and all was quiet.

4. "Help!" the spider called. "Help! Help!"

   "Who's that calling 'Help!'?" asked a voice almost in her ear.

   "It's me, a poor spider," the spider replied. "Who is there?"

   "I'm a fly you were going to eat, just a few minutes ago. We're both in this thing together."

   "Oh!" cried the spider, "am I glad to hear you! What's happened do you suppose? Is it the end of the world?"

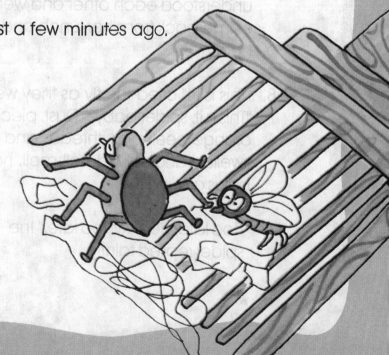

"Oh no!" said the fly. "We've just been eaten by something bigger than both of us. That's the way things are. Spiders eat flies, birds eat spiders; cats eat birds. It's either eat or get eaten in this life."

5. The spider was silent for a while.

   "I didn't think it would end like this," she said at last. "Now I feel sorry for all the flies I've eaten in the past. If only I could get out of here I'd live my life differently, I can tell you."

   "Funny you should say that," said the fly. "I was thinking the same thing. If only I could have my time over again, I'd be a different fly. I'd stay away from rubbish heaps and I'd never walk all over someone's meat with dirty shoes on again."

6. "I'd learn to eat berries," the spider declared. "I'd drink honey like a butterfly. I'm not really an insect myself, but I'd learn insect ways."

   "Come to think, spider baby," the fly said. "I don't suppose a fly and a spider ever had a chance to understand each other before. We've never had the chance to talk together as we're talking now."

7. And they went on talking together in the smothering darkness of the dustbin. They promised to start a school where spiders and insects understood each other and were loving and kind. Then the woman came back from her lunch and emptied the dust onto the compost heap.

8. "This is it!" cried the fly as they were taken and shaken up and down. "This is it, spider baby." Dust, pieces of paper, bread crumbs, scraps of orange peel, pins, threads and fluff swelled and swirled pell-mell, holus bolus around them.

   "Too late, dear fly, too late," the spider replied faintly.

9. But it wasn't too late! When the spider recovered from her faint she found herself bruised, but otherwise well and strong on the compost heap. She stretched her legs. They were all there. She set to work and made a new web. Just as she finished it she saw a fly sitting on a leaf, cleaning his wings with his hind legs and watching her.

10. "Is that you, dear fly?" she asked hopefully.

    "Is that you, spider baby?" replied the fly.

    "I've just finished making the prettiest web," the spider went on. "It's a new sort of peaceful web. Come and see it."

    "It looks a lot like the last one," the fly replied. "I think I'll stay here."

    "But fly – we're friends now," the spider pleaded. "All the wicked past is forgotten. Don't you remember our plans, our dreams?"

    "I haven't forgotten," the fly replied. "But it was dark and dusty then, and it's bright and sunny now. And I am a fly and, after all, spider baby, you are a spider. I'm off."

    "Where are you going?" shrieked the spider.

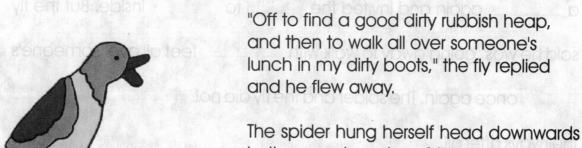

"Off to find a good dirty rubbish heap, and then to walk all over someone's lunch in my dirty boots," the fly replied and he flew away.

The spider hung herself head downwards in the exact centre of her new web. "It's terrible the way some people forget their promise of being loving and friendly. And he was so fat and delicious looking too. Never mind. There'll be another one along soon."

"It's terrible the way some people forget their promise of being loving and friendly. And he was so fat and delicious looking too. Never mind. There'll be another one along soon."

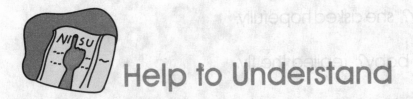

Help to Understand

1. Fill in the blanks after reading the story carefully:

A _____ was caught in a spider's _____ . The _____ was going to _____ it. Just then, a _____ who was cleaning her house swept them into a dustbin. The spider was _____ but the fly was _____ afraid.

Both the insects said they would _____ their ways if they could get out. But as soon as they came out of the _____ , the spider built a _____ again and invited the _____ to _____ inside. But the fly said he was going away to walk with _____ feet all over someone's _____ once again. The spider and the fly did not _____ theirways after all.

2. Answer the following questions:

a. Why did the spider think that the world had come to an end?

b. Was the fly afraid of being inside the dustbin?

3. The spider and the fly talked about a lot of matters. Which of the following points did they agree on? Mark with a (✓) in the space provided :

   a. the world had come to an end ☐

   b. to live life differently ☐

   c. to walk over someone's lunch ☐

   d. to be hopeful ☐

Useful Words

a. Find words in the text, which mean the following.
   The paragraph numbers are given in brackets.
   Each blank must have a single letter.

   a. the home of a spider w __ __ (1)

   b. thrown about from side to side t __ __ __ __ __ (2)

   c. dirt that is thrown out r __ __ __ __ __ __ __ (5)

   d. small , round , soft fruit b __ __ __ __ __ __ (6)

   e. said clearly d __ __ __ __ __ __ __ __ (6)

   f. covering and making it difficult to breathes __ __ __ __ __ __ (7)

   g. a mixture of decaying plants and dung used to make plants

   grow well c __ __ __ __ __ __ __ (7)

b. Look at the pictures below and say what each of these people does. A word from the lesson is given along the margin to help you describe. The paragraph number is in brackets.

Example:

a. caught (1)

This man catches fish.

b) swept (1)

_____

c) emptied (7)

_____

d) shaken (8)

_____

e) flew (10)

This bird _____

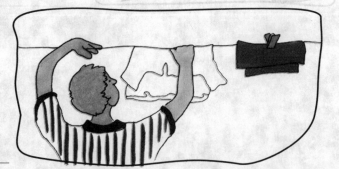

f) hung (11)

This man _____

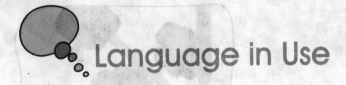

Language in Use

Example:
Oh, said the spider, am I glad to hear you !

Here you have an exclamation with 'am I glad to -----'. You can use 'oh' as an expression of surprise. Look at these pictures. Use 'Oh ' and complete the exclamatory sentences.

Example:

Oh, what a fierce animal !

_____ what colourful _____

_____ strong _____

_____ what cold _____

_____ what a gentle _____

Before You Write

Discuss with a partner. Decide what you want to do / not to do in the New Year.

The following expressions will help you while discussing your points.

I should take care not to _____

I am going to _____

I think I must / I must not _____

It would be wonderful if I could _____

I will if I could _____

I hope to be able to _____

Now Write

My New Year Resolution

Here is a picture of your room. Write a paragraph about your New Year resolution to keep it clean. Find one or two expressions from para 8 of the story to describe it.

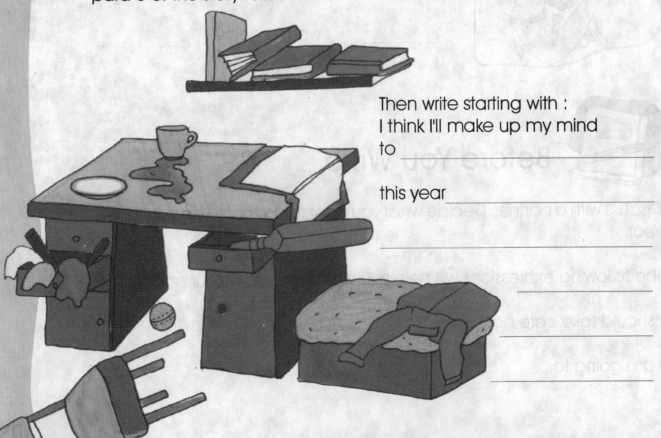

Then write starting with :
I think I'll make up my mind
to _____

this year _____

_____

_____

Game Time

You have some words in the story, which describe the inside of the dustbin. Example: dark, soft, dusty.

Now, play this game with a partner. Blindfold your partner. Give him / her an object. Ask him / her to describe how it feels and what it is.

Example: Paper

It feels smooth.
It is flat.
I think it is paper.

Allow 3 guesses. Then you take your turn at guessing.